Milet Publishing
Smallfields Cottage, Cox Green
Rudgwick, Horsham, West Sussex
RH12 3DE England
info@milet.com
www.milet.com
www.milet.co.uk

First English–Spanish edition published by Milet Publishing in 2013

ISBN 978 1 84059 800 1

Original Turkish text written by Erdem Seçmen
Translated to English by Alvin Parmar and adapted by Milet

Illustrated by Chris Dittopoulos
Designed by Christangelos Seferiadis

Printed and bound in Turkey by Ertem Matbaası

My Bilingual Book

Sight
La vista

English–Spanish

Milet

How do we see colors on a butterfly's wings?

¿Cómo percibimos los colores de las mariposas?

Let's think about how we see things . . .

Vamos a aprender cómo vemos las cosas.

Our eyes show us everything, like faces,

Con los ojos podemos verlo todo: acciones,

colors, actions, places . . .

caras, colores, lugares, situaciones . . .

Giraffe has a coat of brown spots on yellow.

La piel de la jirafa es negra y amarilla.

Watch him bend to say hello!

Mira cómo saluda a la cebra... ¡qué maravilla!

Our eyes can show our feelings.

Nuestros ojos reflejan nuestros sentimientos.

We see Panda's eyes are smiling.

Los del panda parecen sonreír contentos.

To see, we need more than our eyes.

De noche necesitamos luz para poder mirar.

We need light at night to help us spy.

Los ojos solos no atinan en la oscuridad.

Owl can see in a different way.

El búho puede ver de otra manera

Even in the dark, he can spot his prey.

y atrapar a su presa cuando menos se lo espera.

Seeing through glasses? Now I'm perplexed!

Mira el conejo, con su aspecto inteligente.

When our eyes need help, we give them specs!

Si no ves muy bien, debes llevar unos lentes.

Tears are not only for sad or happy,

Lágrimas de tristeza, lágrimas de alegría,

they help keep our eyes moist and healthy.

también mantienen al ojo sano todo el día.

Our eyelids spread our tears when we blink,

Dormimos, parpadeamos, guiñamos pícaramente;

and we use them to sleep and to wink!

los párpados nos protegen los ojos naturalmente.

We close our eyes when we're asleep in bed,

Por la noche, cuando el sueño nos vence,

but in our dreams, we may see orange, green, red . . .

soñamos a todo color: rojo, naranja, verde . . .